Joining Your First Job? Things you must know before joining your first workplace !

I0406639

CONTENTS

Prologue

It's a new Beginning. Totally Fresh out of college, with a lot of aspirations, along with my graduation degree and I felt as if I was all ready to enter the world of realities and a constant voice of my College Principal kept resonating in my head - "It's the survival for the fittest". It looked to me like I was ready to outfit the best formal attire out of my wardrobe as I wanted to look the best of me at my first day at work.

Inspired by this thought - **"Be Sincere."**

Because, being sincere is the virtue which communicates and acts in accordance with our choices, feelings, ideology, the thought-process and our ambitions. One has to look at his / her career from his/her own point of view. It indeed is very important aspect for every individual.

At this point I am thinking about my first job. Starting my career as a whole was more or less similar to my first day at College – There's bound to be an anxiousness and a constant excitement in equal measures.

It is in the month of June when most of the colleges commences with a fresher's batch every year. So many dreams starts afresh. Pursuing education that suits for each one of us as an individual, starts from college. This is still a learning phase, where our parent's takes care of the rest, nothing to worry about other than preparing for examinations and assignments for every semester.

Well, all's well that ends well if one has the dream job being offered towards the end of the final semester. As one receives an offer letter stating most important three words - "You are hired."

One feels the biggest accomplishment is achieved. But it is just a baby step for a journey full of surprises.

This mere thought in itself for me was overwhelming as it's indeed my first step into the grown-up attitude towards the outside world. I will be earning on my own.

And that's when one tends to think that the journey from college to career will be picture perfect for a perfect life.

But here's few things one should know – in fact all in a nut shell one has to know! This first step in itself is the major path that will drive your future. And making this decision - It's definitely not at all easy.

With this book let me share my knowledge and experience that might change your perspective to start your career journey all afresh and definitely in sync with the choices you would like to make as my reader.

1. BE A LEARNER

I would like to quote Anthony J. D'Angelo who said -

"Develop a passion for learning. If you do, you will never cease to grow. "

Starting a new job is exciting and is equally stressful! You're embarking on a new journey of your life that will bring you another step closer to adulthood & independence. You will become more responsible and social to some extent. So here you are at the very first step towards building an amazing career path. It all begins with your very first job. And being open to learning new things will expand your horizon to amazing   experiences.

How will you define as learning something new, or rather how would you understand that you have learnt something new?

Well it all starts from **"Own it like Day One"**. Make sure the learning curve you start from your **"Day One"** is adding some amount of value to your   skillset.

Consider every day you begin as your "Day One" to work towards your success and to find your happiness from   it   each   and   every   day.

It does looks too fancy but at the same time your first job can be extremely nerve-racking as you have already been through and appearing for those campus recruitment processes and competing against all odds to be the chosen one. It all starts from the time you enter the race by the interview process, sometimes being in those long queue's for walk-in interviews , filling the application form and signing on the contract to be in terms with the organization, the first day onboard session and about the awareness of the company's culture and the environment.

Post the entire selection process – when you get selected and being provided with the joining date. You wait eagerly for your very first day at work with a lot of excitement and confusion. How will this day be ? How will your journey be from this place onwards?

Be prepared from your "day one ". Be prepared for employee orientation .

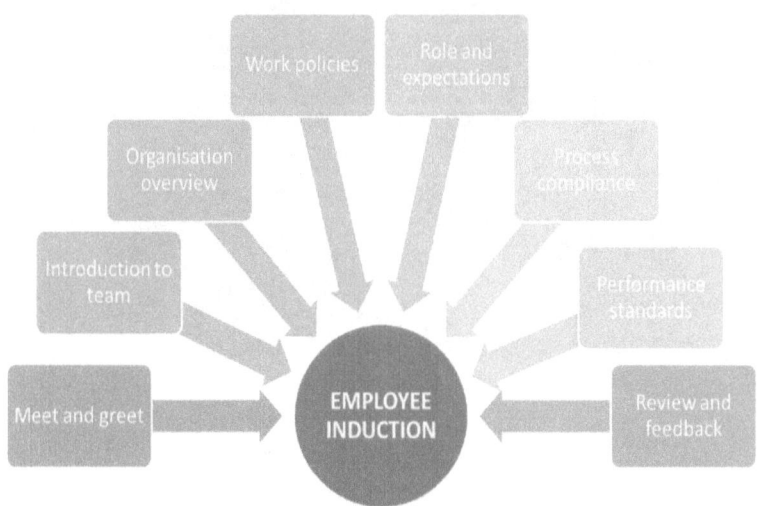

It's also called the **induction program** where you will be meeting and greeting your leader / boss, your fellow colleagues and you will be taken to the work space showing you your future work area.

As it all may seem – too overwhelming to some it also can be really scary at the first job.

Learning so many things at once is too much of information download but remember it's the day from where you start a journey of learning – continuously.

Trust me I have felt the same and sometimes even wondered all those years invested in school and college was mere a degree, to be well qualified to get these opportunities but education is not over with a graduation / post-graduation degree.

" Learning is the key ingredient for Growing .. Learn to Grow .. Grow to Lead and Lead to Inspire .. "

Mentioning about learning process as it is a continuous effort each and every day. I would like to quote an Italian sculptor, painter, architect, poet, and engineer of the High Renaissance who exerted an unparalleled influence on the development of Western art.

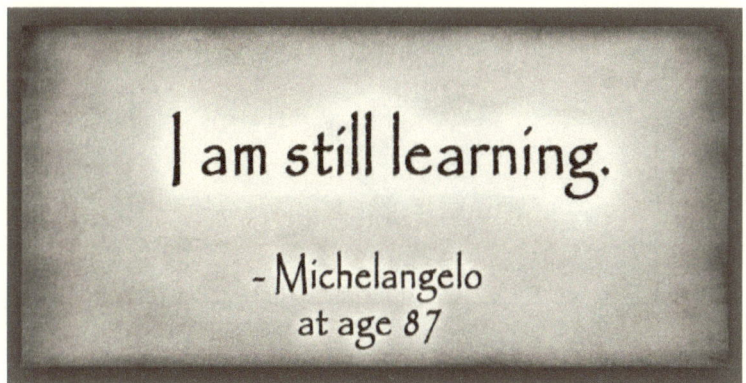

I am still learning.

- Michelangelo
at age 87

And there is so much more to know each and every day at work from everyone. It's natural to want to stop learning when you've learned everything you need to for your current position. However, this can make the job boring really fast and could potentially prevent you from being considered for another position or promotion. After having spent good amount of time in a particular job role - as an individual you need to identify -What's next?

Be curious to acquire more knowledge. Learn to adapt to different kinds of styles many individuals have who surround you at your work on a daily basis.

I must tell you, we all have this learning curve. A learning curve is a graphical representation of the increase of learning , with experience - make sure yours is not a "steep learning curve". It should be more like an S-curve.

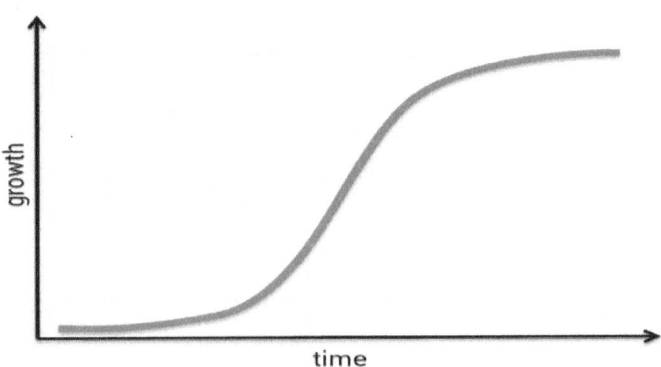

It's really tough to face an uphill saturation - to grow from this stagnancy move your learning curve graph with new ideas, practices efficiency and implementing them. The ultimate goal is always to survive to be at a better place at some   point   in   the   future. Learning how to do tasks outside of your job description shows the upper management not only your initiative, but that you can be reliable and willing to do more. If someone from another department within the company is unable to complete a task or job, management can rely on you to potentially assist in the given situation. Or in someone's absence, as you have already learnt the cross-functional skills you can be a backup to have the task completed within   the   desired   timeframe.

This can also give you an advantage for another position or promotion. You can even potentially encourage your manager to give you a raise!

"STILL LEARNING .. GROWING CONTINUOUSLY .

There are a ton of things to keep in mind before starting your first job, and a lot you learn from in job career guidance cell in college – they offer such courses, and even from your own family members who has the real time experience. Preparing well in advance, thinking which job would suit your passion right from the beginning can mold your career in favorable direction, because there are few who also all end up starting they wish they had done something different   or   had   known   all   this   before.

There is no harm in starting over –but what if you have

things already in hand that could give you a fair chance to "**START AFRESH**" ?

It will help you determine your career objective and clearer goals for your future.

So, make sure you are not in desperate situation to grab any job that comes to your way. Do your bit of **self-actualization** (It simply means the realization or fulfilment of one's talents and potentialities, what you are capable of , especially considered as a drive or need present in each and every individual) in advance, be aware of your skills sets and your dreams, learn those required skill sets and do not lose hope. It's really important to be aware of the difference between being proactive and being desperate. Become familiar with the current business etiquette. Seriously, a lot has been changed over all these years. It's more about adaptability and knowledge that you possess takes you to the places.

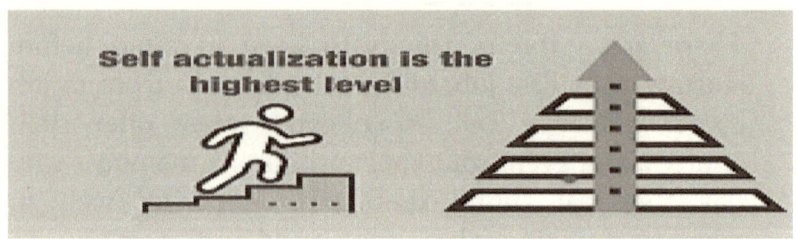

Get involved with your work with passion. Re-iterating few famous words as an example here-

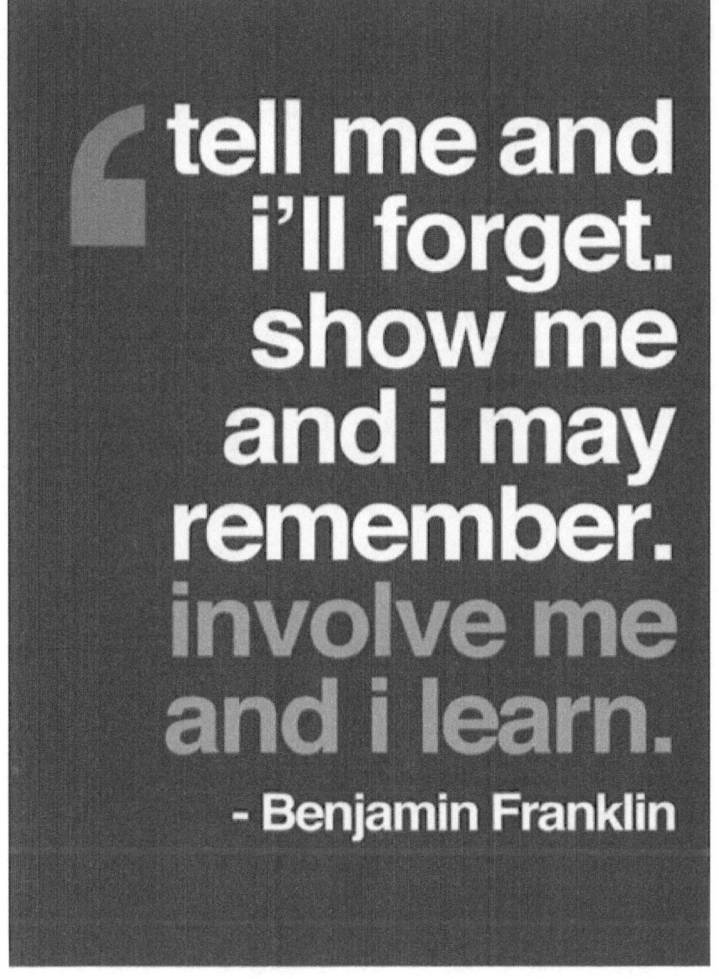

Now comes the crucial part in your first job – your training days – everyone calls it "The Honeymoon period "yet do know it well in advance - that whatever you learn during your training in your first days / weeks be proactive, be curious, and don't be shy about asking any questions or seeking clarifications. It's your right to do so. Trust me, it is better to ask your doubts then and there rather than risk messing it up. In the end, you'll save a lot of time for you and for someone else present in the team, someone else might also have the same question and by simply asking your question you are helping the team work more efficiently.

Be curious to learn and increase your knowledge about the terminologies used within the organization. And by doing so you will be showcasing your independence, your initiatives, your talent, you're potential within the organization.

I would like to re-iterate what **Albert Einstein** had said

" Education is not the learning of facts , but training of the mind to think. "

This adds to the learning-curve you will create through your first work experience. Make sure it is worth sharing.

Be ready to face it all , see through it and progress with it in both terms - Professional & Personal.

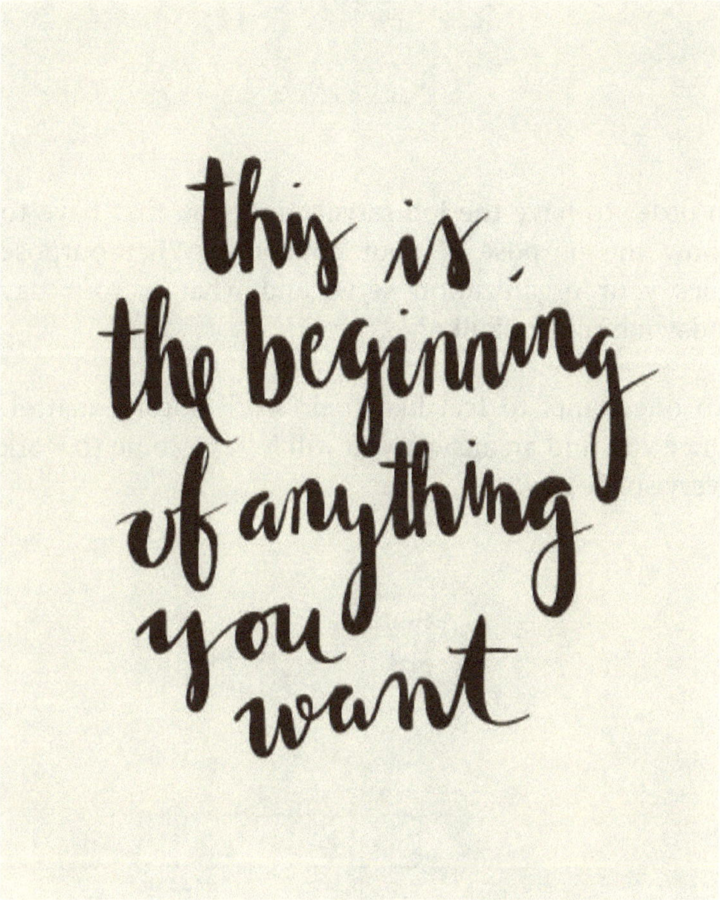

this is the beginning of anything you want

-unknown

This is where the professional journey begins .

2.HAPPINESS @ WORKPLACE :D

In order to have the job satisfaction, you first have to know the purpose of your company. What purpose does your organization serve and what is your day today job role look like?

No one wants to feel like their work doesn't matter. Once you find an answer you will love to come to work every single day.

HAPPIER,
MORE ENGAGED,
MORE SUCCESSFUL
AT WORK

- **Embracing happy work culture** - It implies to happy employees by having more engagement, more career progression discussions, more opportunities and more smiles at work.

- **Cultivate good relationships** - This talks about how we earn each other's trust for building grater team bonding. Connecting with each-other drives healthy work culture. Motivates individuals to co-work. This helps in finding opportunities and solutions at much faster pace.

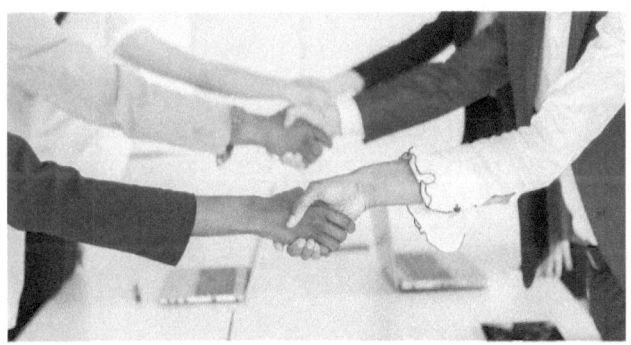

- **Embracing and inspiring employee autonomy** - This help in building a team with integrity and in turn opens an opportunities for greater ideas to be explored for continuous improvement.

- **Practicing flexibility** - A bigger aspect towards finding work-life balance. This gives an improved ability to be responsible. One such example is Work From Home. There are situations where-in our family needs our presence and yet work is equally important-after all its our bread and butter. So, to tackle such situation and have the balance in chaos WFH is being flexible towards employees personal responsibility. It definitely provides job satisfaction for being with family in need.

WORK FROM HOME

- **Communicating purpose & passion** - Communication is the most important aspect in any professional world. And having transparency in the communication will keep the show going and all will be on the same page. This will definitely drive Passion for the work one do and will in turn be helpful in job satisfaction one need.

Working hard for something we don't care about is called stress. Working hard for something we love is called passion.

-Simon Sinek

You Might learn the technology and rest of the technicalities at your new workplace with the time yet having a strong interpersonal skill from the start can take you to the places right from the very beginning. From the early stage of your career this one skill will help you get along with your team and your manager. This builds mutual respect and credibility at workplace.

It is an important ingredient in many aspects. Like Interpersonal skills directly implies to treating people with clear communication, with empathy, with respect, positivity and with etiquette.

I would like to re-iterate one of my favorite quote here –

> *"Ordinary People with extraordinary motivation can achieve remarkable performance through a pattern of arduous work and study called deliberate practice"*
>
> - Professor K. Anders Ericsson

Then why not begin with this kind of practice right from the very start ? - Right !

Make the beginning itself adds to the wonderful journey ahead.

Go to work with the same happy zeal each and every day.

Here's few example what an employee says and what is the reason they love their job. As it all contributes towards job satisfaction -

- ✓ *"Everyone is supportive in their own ways and always willing to provide their help and guidance and experience to accomplish the team goals.*

- ✓ *"Every team member has a smile on their face. This is a great place to work."*

- ✓ *"The company has a business model that is unsurpassed and their ethics and morals are among the elite."*

- ✓ *"I feel that I am supported in any decisions that I make and that my co-workers genuinely care about my well-being, both personally and professionally."*

- ✓ *"The work environment I work in is calm and pleasant. My managers have an open door policy and listen to our concerns and provides timely solutions."*

Happy @ Work .. makes a Happy Life !

Joining Your First Job? Things you must know before joining your first workplace !

3. COPING WITH DIVERSE WORK ENVIRONMENT

By definition Diversity simply means - a range of different things that are seen together.

We all are aware of Diversity. And it is the prime focus in every organization. Diversity in itself is vast and yet interlinks a lot of factors that surround work culture.

Diversity by definition is in itself is a collaboration of mixed attributes that contain different elements and can include having employees of different age groups, gender, religion, ethnicity, culture, physical ability, sexual orientation, work experience, religious beliefs, and educational qualification, from different countries and so on.... So you are not a lone soul in this working environment, you are a team working in collaboration within the organization.

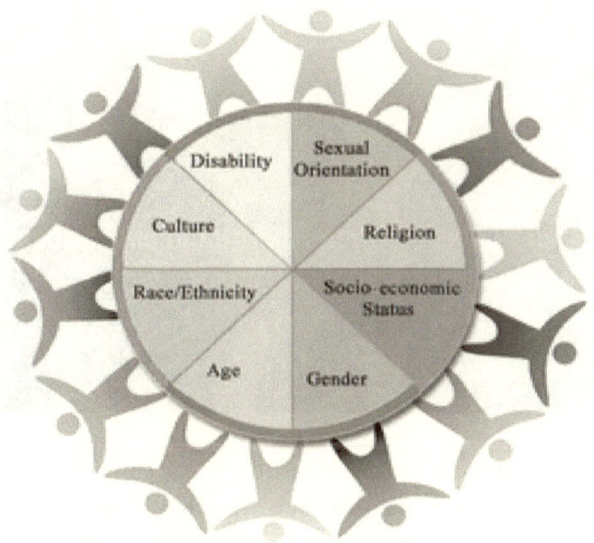

You will be a part of diverse culture were your will be taught about team bonding. It directly implies to building a culture that dwells on working together, still be able to say your individual thoughts out loud without hesitation and with respect and acceptance by others.

Diversity again is correlated to Learning –and here you can learn to co-learn & co-operate. This routes us to team-building activities and how team works on various aspects called – Collaboration, Active listening, Emotional intelligence, Conflict resolution, compromise and earning each other's trust or Building Credibility.

I would to mention this quote which out writes the exact meaning for the word " Diversity " and why it is so important- by Stephan R. Covey

"Strength lies in differences, not in similarities"
- Stephen R. Covey

The way I see it – it's a good thing. How can this be inculcated within a diverse team?

Try moving out of your comfort zone and make your workplace lively and active by knowing who you work with. One has to know what constitutes to the diverse workplace. Who is the part of the system. Focus on the larger picture here. In fact you can find out who is good at what?

You need to indulge in prioritize communication at workplace be it about the process updates, policies, procedures, any safety rules, or any other information one should be aware of as an employee should be communicated by effective means. Treat your co-worker or fellow colleague with respect and their individual space.

If everyone is thinking alike,
then someone isn't thinking.

– GEORGE S. PATTON

Give accolades to the deserving individual and be involved in any kind of team related activities. Share your ideas and perspective with one-another or with the leader via a good mode of commination – like written email. This could help you get the credit of your idea and would avoid any confrontation. In case of any ambiguity about any situation always seek assistance from your leader/ boss or his/her boss. Make sure you follow the hierarchy – be aware of the hierarchy. In case there is a need to skip this levels make sure you do have a valid point to put forward to.

The ultimate goal of Diversity is beautifully described in the below mentioned quote -

> *Confidence isn't walking into a room with your nose in the air, and thinking you are better than everyone else.*
> *It's walking into a room and not having to compare yourself to anyone else in the first place.*

-unknown

4. SKILLS YOU NEED TO KNOW BEFORE STARTING YOUR FIRST JOB !

Here's the challenging aspect, beyond college life -

" Facing the real world. "

You are an important part of a future team and your accountability towards your work matters at every level. We learnt a lot in college, still the courses back in college doesn't teach about - so many literal aspects to   simple   questions?

HOW TO BE ON BOARD ?

HOW TO MANAGE YOUR TIME WELL?

HOW TO COPE UP WORKING WITH VARIETY OF PEOPLE?

HOW TO WORK TOWARDS PROGRESS AND GETTING A PROMOTION ?

WHAT'S NEXT?

WHEN & WHERE IS THE NEXT MEETING?

WHERE SHALL I FIND ANSWERS TO THOSE QUESTIONS? HOW TO JUGGLE ON VARIED PROJECTS?

HOW TO MULTITASK- NAVIGATING THROUGH VARIOUS DEPARTMENTS /FACILITIES ONE NEED TO BE AT THE TOP OF YOUR WORK ?

-Jyoti Kumari

It all matters. But here's the question - How will you know all this unless you have experienced the same all by yourself? Yes, all such questions and queries needs to be addressed. Know who to contact in case you have any questions? Know Your surroundings.. and slowly you will get all your questions answered. It's called **Q&A.**

Well I have few topics to cover - which will get you onboard in starting the first job.

There are plenty of things that you get to know - Right from office campus to training facilities , from getting to start to work , to know about the codes of conduct , about dress code , about people around , from work culture to infinite things that are **All NEW ?**

Know your colleagues

To start afresh - Get some air. Find similar hobbies and probe/ask questions to one another. Get along. Introduce yourself. Go get a coffee/tea together. Go for break. You will encounter different persons at work on a daily basis. You need to learn as in how to deal with such people and their aspects of your office culture.

Starting from boarding your office cab to work sitting with colleagues at different levels , from home to reaching office campus, from security check to the receptionist, from fellow peers to your boss/Leader and so on and so forth. It's important for you to be aware of who to reach out to in what kind of situation.

You will need to understand how people from different background and generation co-work. Hence learn to get along and dwell a good professional relation at work. Keep your work and personal life separate.

Be professional and ethical in work place environment to encourage a healthy workplace for all.

" Build your network. Connect often and be a part of a progressive work habit. "

-Jyoti kumari

THE FACE GAME :

This game is very famous in most of the organizations and is usually conducted during various induction sessions as a quick introduction round and simply to get to know the fellow colleagues.

How many coworkers can you recognize in 30 seconds?

Try the FaceGame

Try to know and remember who your fellow colleagues are. Go grab a coffee together and find about each other more during a lunch break. Know who do you work with and build your network at workplace.

Competence & Responsibility

Know   how   to   be   on   track   in   the   race?

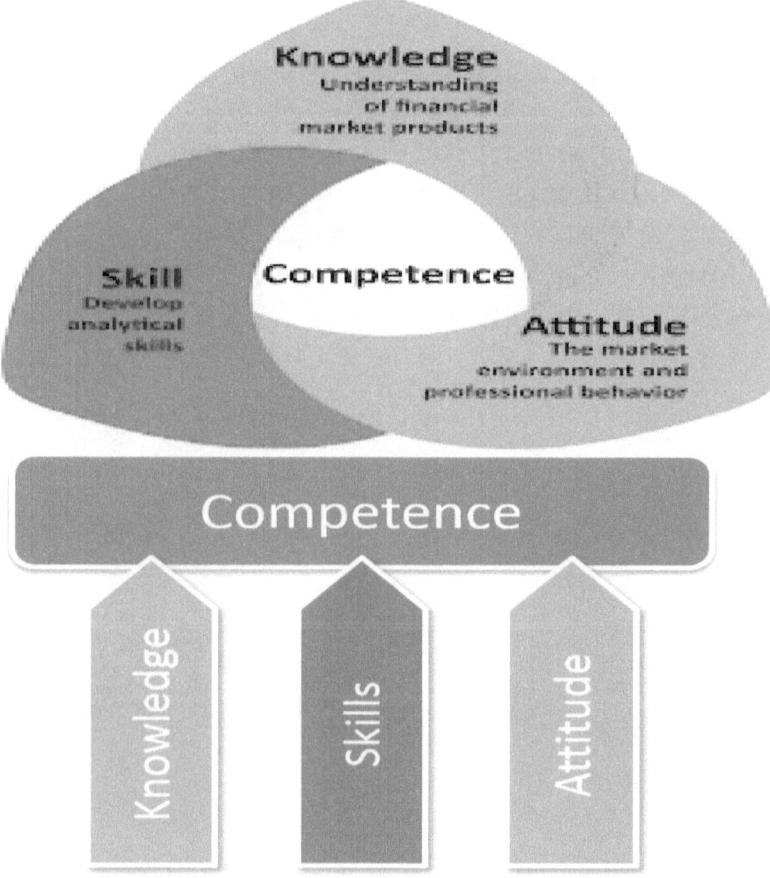

It's not the chase on the cricket field instead it takes a lot of pragmatic scenarios to go along to be in the race. You need to deal with things with a lot of sensibility and realistically while sitting in a through the day to get going and you won't even know how time flies while you get to be doing your daily job. Make sure you find time to get a breather to think out of the box and be innovative and creative in your thoughts to be part of the race.

It's a tough chase out there. It could be challenging, could be repetitive and you might feel you are being monotonous after a point in time. You could be cutting the edge through a tough competition by being visible with the right influence amongst the crowd. Yet it takes a lot to be competitive. Along with competence comes the responsibility.

RESPONSIBILITY

starts with *me.*

Your schedule for any given day will already be defined and either being on time or ahead of time is a good way to represent your ownership and responsibility towards your work.

You need to be on time every single day. These responsibilities might extract some extra times from your week offs or extended working hours. You need to understand and learn to differentiate to commit or say a polite no.

There is nothing wrong in saying a no instead of committing to something that could not fulfilled. Still understand one thing here you must give importance to every petty work that comes your way. Always remember that you are in a fast-paced work culture where you will have to deal with complex tasks and it requires great amount of focus.

Do not lose your focus, however overlooking a few determinable factors could depend upon the eye for the detail that is required for you to proceed with the task efficiently. Here's where your enthusiasm is the key element.

Being responsible is also directly related to your personality. How do you look? Or I can rather say how you represent yourself determines your companies image, while at work or outside work. Groom yourself and create a persona that is admirable or people would like to look up to you. This makes you venerable in all ways adds to your self-esteem and an image to carry forward.

You will be accountable for your meetings, your emails, your workplace hygiene and your timely projects and of course for your work. In any business, your work affects others and in turn it's crucial for you to know being responsible or delegating your task in your absence can take care of the situation appropriately.

Presentation skills and Public speaking is again a tedious task. You must learn how to present efficiently and effective in front of your client, boss or fellow colleagues.

You need to learn how to put forward your ideas or suggestions in any meetings. Make sure at work you present well with good amount of sample data to back up your statement.

Like you could collect relative questions, its interpretations and be also ready to face any difference in opinion and how to handle that situation without stammering in a team.

Competence & responsibility works hand in hand. Your responsivity towards your work drives your ability to perform and that in-turn results in successful accomplishment.

-Jyoti Kumari

Handling constructive feedback

In business world a very commonly used terminology is feedback. A feedback is nothing but someone within the organization who has any opinion on your work could approach you directly or via an email.

It could be both a positive or negative.

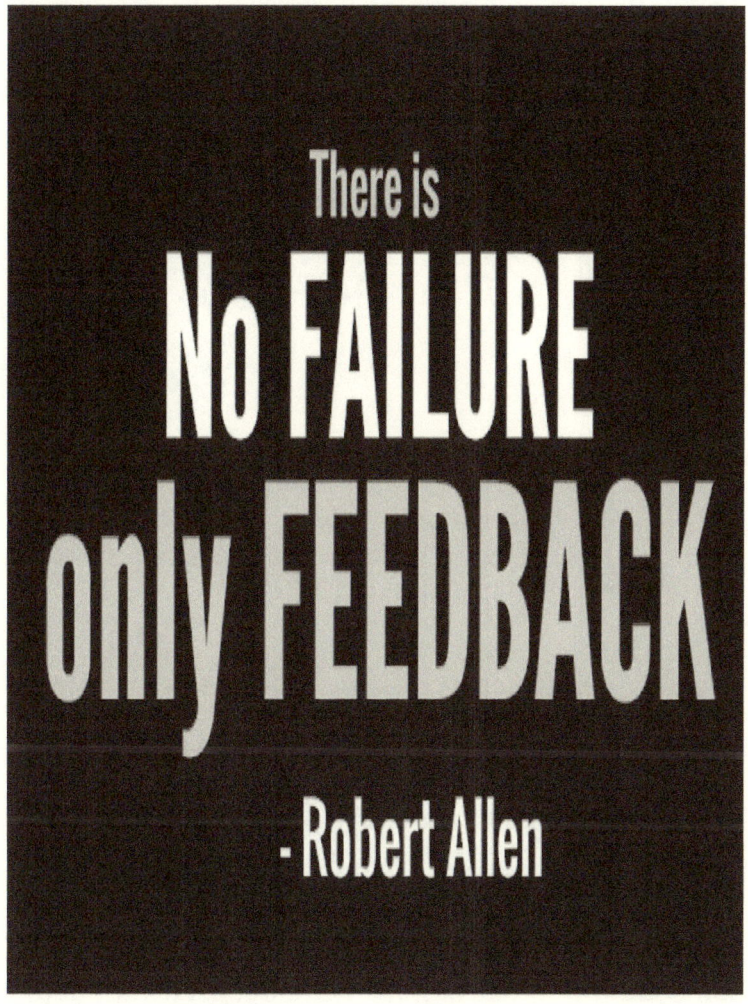

Well, this is where you will need to inculcate and incorporate yourself into understanding your areas of strengths and weaknesses. Identify them earlier and work towards taking any given feedback to be taken constructively for the betterment of your work. Now a day's people have an option to take classes on business and business etiquette.

Most commonly used feedback model is called an **SBI feedback model**.

Situation
Describe the situation. Be specific about when and where it occurred.

Behavior
Describe the observable behavior. Don't assume you know what the other person was thinking.

Impact
Describe what you thought or felt in reaction to the behavior.

These were few basic tips that one should know - someone who is starting his/her career. This will let to know as in - how should you get yourself ready for this world of the unknown?

And face the realities with confidence. You can't know everything about a workplace until you get in there but learning some of these skills and lessons before you start your first job will prepare you well and help you excel more quickly.

*Feedback provides
the key to betterment
in terms of quality
product & services.*

-Jyoti Kumari

5. DYS – DISCOVER YOUR STRENGTHS !

Strength = Potential skill sets
+ Confidence

Always look for whats the best that defines you. When providing context for your strengths, address the specific qualities that qualify you for the job role you are being hired for.

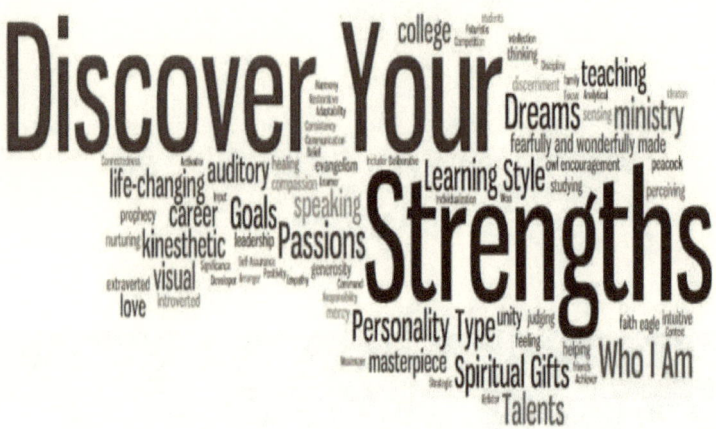

SOME KEY POINTS FOR STRENGTHS DISCOVER YOURS !

Ability to prioritize

To be able to prioritize your tasks you need make a list of things we have planned to do. Categorize them in **Urgent Vs Important attributes**. Look at the equation and assess them as per the value. Find out how much effort you need to put on each one of the tasks. Make sure you are adaptable and flexible as well and know when to be stringent about the your priorities. Always make sure you have created a written agenda for timely follow up 's and easily accessible anywhere anytime.

Attention to detail

This in specific drives your eye to detail ability, how much are you aware or thorough & accurate about the tasks you would like to accomplish ? Why is it so important ? Because the more you pay attention , the less are the chances of any mistakes which in turn will drive success in the tasks.

Communication

The most important mode of exchanging any kind of information with respect to work is communication. how effectively you communicate, defines you at work. There are 4 types of communication - Verbal, Non-verbal , Written & Visual. Be aware of 7 C's of effective communication : - **Completeness, Conciseness, Consideration, Clarity, Concreteness, Courtesy & Correctness.** (from Management study) –

Interpersonal skills

Well this is equally important because it requires multiple skills at once - like are you a team player , are you empathetic , do you possess leader like qualities. , are you actively listening , dependability in some situations & Independent in some situation, being responsible. Do you have ability to motivate people around you ? Do you have enough patience ? How flexible are you? All these put together constitute your interpersonal skills.

Punctuality

Simply being on time shows your respect for people and their time. And learning to be punctual makes you everyone's favorite. If you inculcate this habit , you will be successful. Because , Punctuality directly implies to your attitude towards your behavior and not missing on things during trainings/meetings which others might miss just because they are late.

Self-confidence

Taking control of things on your own is a lot of work as well. This does rely on the fact that -   how confident are you about yourself? It includes a lot of things - How do you look ?   Are you a positive thinker ? Do you know your own self ? How you dress ? Groom yourself and look nice and presentable. Be kind and courteous. Focus on things, Smile and greet people around. Volunteer whenever any initiative taken. Increase your knowledge. Do things from your bucket-list. Make one and then explore them. Keep your desk tidy and clean. Stay active and enthusiastic.

Soft skills

This constitutes the very basic skills at required to be a part of corporate world. Like Good communication, problem-solving and decision making capability , positive attitude , your emotional intelligence , willingness to learn , self-management & your role within a team.

Teamwork

Good team work is nothing but co-operating with each other while working on similar tasks. How strongly all the individual within the teams are connected? It's helpful in solving problem together. One can always build the trust and respect for one another. Always encourage being social. Recognition within the team enhances the team's performance.

Working under pressure

Understanding how to react in a given situation deals with your taking the load concept. How well can you manage stress? Always have a perspective in place. Rise above the work pressure, in fact learn to stay above the line. Make sure you are not missing on your timely breaks. Focus on work and know the timelines well in advance.

Enthusiastic/Passionate/Driven

Being enthusiastic in itself is an amazing skill. It provides amazing benefits for the individual. It simply inspires others to be someone like them. You will be passionate and driven with this skill set. You will love what you do. And this love what you do attitude will take you far in an organization.

Collaborative

 This again enables an individual to work together to achieve business purpose together. One can collaborate in many forms like via interacting in real time or available for meetings online , over the phone, emails etc. This simply describes teamwork taken to a higher level. This skill helps in building good employee relationships , in handling conflicts at work and in learning to deal with new situation together.

Analytical thinking

This is a very critical aspect for visualizing your thinking ability. It always requires methodical approach to your thinking out of the box ability. This in turn can help build greater ability to gather , collect , visualize and analyze any information in different forms and via different approaches. This is very helpful in solving complex problems.

Disciplined/Focused

This contributes towards a pattern of behavior where an individual pushes his / her inner power to get into a routine. It's a very healthy practice and coming out of your comfort zone and pushing your boundaries helps you explore more about your own self. - Innovation - The action of being involved in multiple activities to discover new aspects in the same old routine gives birth to innovation. This is present in changing and redefining the current trends to make it count.

Being Creative

Lastly being creative is also the most important aspect in an individual which helps you to be innovative. This helps you in becoming a better problem solver and makes your approach to dealing with different issues in much better ways. This always gives you a new way. Look at things differently.

This could be done by using mind maps. Always carry your idea book along, anytime something comes up write it down. You can always have your own vision board. Explore the unknown and see creativity beyond your imagination. Explore and engage in creative work instead of repetitive work.

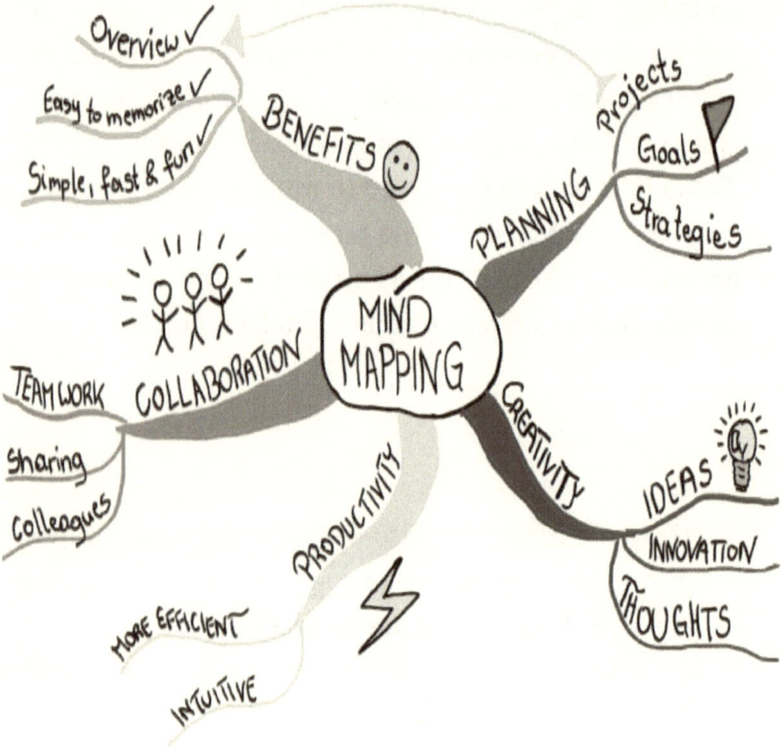

And Now you are ready to be welcomed to face the real World.

◆◆◆

Conclusion

Finally, I would like to conclude this book by telling you the important aspect -

---

"Choosing your career is the most important decision, Make it right for you, because no one knows you better than your own self. "

Make sure you interact with many people who surround you and know their best stories from their first job experience .
Try to find a professional mentor. Someone whom you admire, someone who can guide you through your initial days which can help you transition through your college life to and real-world experience, a mentor who can prepare you for an office environment and help you navigate new situations at work. It will help you through all the different situations that might come your way. All the best for your first job.

MAKE IT COUNT AND BE PREPARED.

*** THANK YOU ***

*Famous writer's quotes added - As an avid reader and I would love to re-iterate few such inspiring quotes.

Remember .. Choosing your career is your choice !

ABOUT THE AUTHOR

Author Jyoti talks about many simple aspect that one has to keep in mind while starting your career journey. This book gives leverage to every reader and clears your perspective for where and how to begin your professional journey. Worked with Google & Facebook, Author talks about what is that thing which drives your passion for work?

You need to follow your passion and evolve with it.

Professional journey is not a perfect picture but what you build while on this journey matters.

Find that Balance and grow with it

True success comes your way when you take action on a daily basis. ***Make it your Habit.***

Yes, Make it your habit to work towards your progress that will help you achieve goals and lets you live the life you've always dreamed of.

In his books, Author Jyoti provides simple aspects that will help every aspiring candidate who is seeking his/her very first job – should be able to decide the purpose and proceed towards the dream job that will help them build their career journey an amazing one right from the very beginning.

So instead of reading over-hyped strategies that rarely work in the real world, be aware of those simple things your need to know even before you enter your professional world. You'll get simple information that can be immediately implemented.

All the best.

Much Love

Jyoti